Foreword

This collection contains work written over the last fifty years, or so. Some of the poems reflect my experiences as a merchant seaman, and some as a teacher.

The poems might be traditional, like the ballad-like, Sailor's Rhyme, or be freely structured, like Tanker Bird, or even experimental, like the englynesque Aneurin Bevan, Politician. Many are humorous, such as My Mum, or tongue-in-cheek or even whimsical, such as Journeys, while others are serious, such as Two Photographs. Some might have a simple before-and-after type of narrative, like that of Hedgehog, and others a more complex type of narrative, like that of Senghenydd; hence the title of the collection: *A Mixed Bag*.

Several of the poems have appeared in publications (some no longer extant) such as *Envoi, Viewpoints, The Seafarer*, the *Western Mail*, the *Anglo-Welsh Review*, the *New Welsh Review*, *Roundyhouse*, and the annual anthologies of the Tuesday Poetry Group based in the Swansea Uplands.

The photograph was taken by Ian George of Visual Photo Graphics, Loughor, and the illustrations were done by local Llanelli/Swansea artist, Tony Paultyn.

BRETT HAYES, 2015

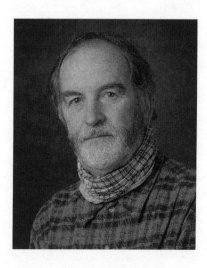

Contents

Simple Bread-making

Sift into a bowl a pound of wholemeal flour
To make one loaf or eight small rolls, at least.

Add a teaspoon each of salt and sugar;
Blend with a warm, frothy leaven of yeast.

Stir in more tepid water, as needed,
Then flour a board and lightly knead the mix.

Plump the dough into a two-pound loaf-tin
(With softened butter generously greased)

And leave to rise, covered, in a warm place,
Until its girth by twofold has increased.

Slash the top and bake in a hot oven
For thirty-five minutes at gas mark six.

Turn out carefully with an oven-cloth
And tap the bottom of the loaf to test

If it's done. Stand the bread on a wire-rack,
For the crumb to have time to cool and rest,

Then, knife in hand, with a decisive thrust,
Cut down through the crisp, cragged outcrop of crust.

Prose-poem on Cawl

Sweat the onion and the garlic with melted butter in a pan, then remove and set aside. Sear in sizzling batches the seasoned salt-marsh lamb, and do to this likewise.

Fry the carrot, swede and parsnip until they golden all in one. Put the mixture in a casserole. Sprinkle with rosemary, sage and thyme, then pour the hot stock over and simmer slowly till it's done.

My Mum . . .

My mum would preach the old adage:
Never let good food go to waste;
So I'd clear my plate of cabbage,
Though the dog didn't like the taste.

I was told . . .

I was told that a foal is long in the tooth,
That liars always tell the truth,
And that Genghis Khan was never uncouth,
That gluttons do not over-eat,
That butchers give away their meat,
And that fingers grow on the ends of your feet.

I heard of a pagan going to mass,
Of a horse that said it didn't like grass,
And a donkey that swore it wasn't an ass,
Of a cat that fell in love with a mouse,
Of the Glorious Twelfth without a grouse,
And of firemen trying to burn a house.

I saw three apples make a pair,
A potato rub its eyes and stare,
And the Devil read from The Book of Prayer,
But oddest of all, I must declare –
Despite the fact that I wasn't there –
I saw a bald man comb his hair.

The Spider

"The mutant spider had vanished from sight,"
Said detective inspector Gavinda Ghose,
"Though its web was found near the bedroom-light,
Concealed in a crack by the ceiling-rose.
On the hammock below lay Miss Hepplewhite
Who seemed roused by shock from a deep repose,
For her eyes were staring, transfixed by fright,
And her corpse curled up in a foetal pose,
With no mark on her face save a tiny bite
And a trace of blood on the tip of her nose.
But strangest of all," said inspector Ghose,
"Is that something entered the morgue that night –
Though how it had done so nobody knows –
To look for the deceased and wrap her tight
In a shroud of silk from her head to her toes."

Tanker Bird

Head back, as if singing, beak half-open
And splintering with the heat, the bird lay.
It seemed elegant from far off, sitting
As though cradled in sleep upon a nest,
Yet neither twigs nor leaves were near
To shade or shield it. Only the wide flat
Acres of a steel deck, with valve-wheels,
Gas-vents and rows of bowelling pipeline.
Tar-black. Diagrammatic. And unchanging.
Except where this small dark bird, oil-
-stiffened and withered in claw, lay, its eyes
Shrunk pips, and the slender tongue that seemed
Poised, as if to sing, stuck in its throat,
As it kept on spilling dry burnt notes
In a shrivelled pool upon the hot flat deck.

Russian Trawlers

One fine day in the South Atlantic
We sighted them,
Bows sharply raked,
Proceeding south,
Following each other
At the same speed
At exact distances apart.

A pack of lean grey wolves
Hungry
Far from home,
Searching that calm sunlit sea
With a precision
As merciless and cold
As the Siberian winter.

Oiled Seabird

One still, moonless night,
The tide delivered,
Then slipped away secretly –
Leaving an aborted black foetus
At the scene of her surgery.

Frigate

Frigate – gliding secretly
Into mist at twilight
With hardly a sound,
Hardly a light.

The guns are still.
Straight. Unswung.
And not a sailor
Not one, in sight.

It steals away,
Antennae alert,
Trying to prick-out, pin-point,
Something out there in the mist.

A ghostly insect
Trained to seek,
The scanner in its head
Sweeping rhythmically

In cycles,
Tracing flickering white specks
Upon a grey screen
As it moves on

Flailing the soft mist.
Probing. Without hurry.
Its one light
Passing silently.

Sailor's Rhyme

Yesterday we picked him up
All bloated with the brine,
Drowned like a dog and half as swelled
Two days below the Line.

The corpse in linen cloth we swathed
And wound it cool and white,
Sewed tarpaulin round the shroud
And drew the stitching tight.

At dawn, we chalked an old hatch-board
To help the canvas slip,
Carried him slowly to the rail
Ready to leave the ship.

As we stood by, we thought of him
Within the winding-sheet,
An iron bar between his legs
A shackle at his feet,

For each of us was warm with life
Not laid-out cold and dead,
Soon to lie in a lonely grave
Upon the ocean-bed.

The breeze had died and all seemed still
The sea lay flat and calm,
The only sound the captain's voice
Reading aloud a psalm.

And when the service had been read
We slid him out beneath,
Watched him sink and ghost from sight
As bosun pitched a wreath.

Pinups

Tonight I stripped my pinups
From the cabin-wall:
Rid my temple of temptation:
Defiled breasts, desecrated thighs
Long held hallowed through privation.

False goddesses,
They would never live;
Though they smiled and proffered
Their love, they flaunted only
What they could not give.

Having purged my shrine,
I find the wall I have exposed
Is smooth, flat and cold,
And as loveless and bare
As they were.

Dead Pike

Obsolete missile.
Dumped on the river-bank.
Defused.
Due for disposal.
No longer a deterrent
To passing trout
Or moorhen chick
As it slipstreams the current,
Or a presence
That might lie in wait
In sun-dappled shallows
Till its warhead detonate
In an explosion
Of silver minnows.

Lowestoft Fish-dock
(Autumn 1973)

Barrels.
Steel drums.
Ice.
Men with lean eager blades
Gut fish.

Dogfish
Slit round the neck,
Gripped by the head
And torn –
Unzipped tubes
Of pink meat.

Plaice
Planed of fillets
X-rays
Flipped away.

And cod –
Great steelskinned cod –
Barbel-lipped,
Dole-eyed,
Gape like the mouth
Of an open trawl.

Fatstock Show
(Prize Beast)

The steer stands, tethered by rope
To a bar in the pen.
Arraigned. Awaiting trial.

The judge, black bowler-hatted,
Presses strong, hard thumbs
Deep into its haunch –

Feeling the meat beneath,
Appraising the evidence,
The quality of sirloin or rump.

The defendant blinks.
Impassive. Dumb witness
To its own prosecution

Until, slapped on its flank –
The verdict delivered –
It is led from the dock,

Unaware of the sentence
In the gilt medallion
Noosed round its neck.

Chainsaw

By the bare limb of a tree
The chainsaw snarls,
Curling its lip
To reveal white teeth
That will rip
Through bark
To the bone beneath.

Wood-fire

Slowly I eat
    Through blocks of oak,
With lots of heat
    But little smoke.

Feasting on beech,
    My flames leap high;
Fasting on birch,
    They quickly die.

Tree

Does a living tree suffer pain
When saw-teeth rip across the grain
Or numbly shake its twigs and leaves
As one who cuts it down believes?

Could seasoned timber suffer pain
When nails are struck into the grain
And feel the passion of each blow
The cross that once held Christ would know?

Christ's Crucifixion

As he bore the cross to Golgotha,
His bare feet blistered and sore,

Some people at the wayside jeered
And spat at him and swore,

Mocking the so-called King of the Jews
And the crown of thorns that he wore,

Wondering why their jibes and taunts
He seemed patiently to ignore,

Not knowing, as he hung on the cross,
It was they he suffered for .

He . . .

He who fixed Christ to the arms of a cross
    Unmoved by sighs of pain
As iron spikes through hands and feet
    Were nailed into the grain

Found work in the Nazi death-camps
    On the sands of the Polish plain
That dutifully gassed and burnt the Jews
    To the schedule of a train

And never it seems need look too far
    To find such work again.

Vinegar

I am sprinkled with salt on fish and chips
When crisp and golden-fried.

I was held in a sponge against the lips
Of Christ when crucified.

Instructions for Crucifixion

First, saw into two lengths a beam of wood,
One piece equal to the victim's armspan,
The other at least twice as long. They should
Comfortably bear the weight of a man.
The depth of the wood must be sufficient
To take the spikes, which are four in number
And made of steel. (A list of equipment
Is given at the end of this chapter.)
Join the timbers with a cross-halving joint
Or drill two holes and bolt them together.
On completing this, one could bind both hands
And feet to the cross, or as shown on page
Nineteen, clamp them tightly with iron bands –
If this restraint is preferred to cordage.
Thus, with arms extended and made secure,
The legs firmly fettered and feet turned-out,
The nailing may take place. At this juncture,
One might feel some anxiety or doubt,
But the operation is quite simple
To perform. It is crucial, however,
That the spikes, in transfixing each ankle
And wrist, should cause arterial rupture.
Subsequently, one may erect the cross,
Bed it in place and let the victim bleed.
Death will normally ensue through blood-loss
Or asphyxiation, but one might need
To cut the artery in either foot
To expedite this. The sentence should not
Prove difficult to execute if care
Is taken to follow the procedure.
The method is foolproof – despite one case
On record in which death did not occur,
And where, it was alleged, the body rose
From a tomb that was sealed three days before.
But one needn't have reason to worry
If someone survived the bleeding and pain –
The breaking of both legs will guarantee
A problem like that won't arise again.

I broke . . .

I broke in the waters of Mary;
I baptised in the hands of John
girded, thigh-deep, in the Jordan;
I splashed from the nets of Simon Peter.

At a wedding-feast in Cana,
I turned sweetly into wine;
drowned, as they squealed in frenzy,
a herd of Gadarene swine.

I passed through the gills of two fish
blessed with five loaves of barley,
and felt, in the fourth watch of the night,
two feet, weightless, walking upon me.

By the Pool of Siloam,
in spit mixed with clay,
I touched the eyes of a blind man
with the dazzling brightness of day;

betrayed in a kiss at Gethsemane
when Judas had sold his soul;
absolved the conscience of Pilate
as he bathed his hands in a bowl.

I dripped as sweat from Simon of Cyrene
in dust on the road to Golgotha,
and quenched in a sponge of vinegar
the thirst of one thorn-crowned and crucified.

I broke in the waters of Mary;
I broke from the wound in Christ's side.

John Hooper, 1495–1555
(The First Protestant Martyr)

Condemned to death, stripped of his bishopric,
He would choose (though this might seem ironic)
To make his way with the aid of a stick
To the stake, for his joints were arthritic;
And there, by warrant of the Catholic
Queen Mary, to heartfelt cries of public
Grief, perished in flames as a heretic.

John Hoooper
(February 9, 1555)

When, outside the cathedral in Gloucester
On a market-day in February,
They tried to burn bishop John Hooper
With a warrant from Queen Mary,
The wood round the stake being damp, he cried,
"Good people, let me have more fire,
For Christ's sake," then quietly died,
Head bowed, lips moving as if in prayer,
Long before the flames, sweeping higher,
Would turn into ash his soft white hair.

Church-bell

High up in the belfry hung,

Every Sunday I am rung,

Pealing on the Sabbath air,

Chiding with my iron tongue

Those who choose to be elsewhere

Than come to church and kneel in prayer.

●

Medieval Carpenters

The tools they used are familiar,
still, to us: mallet, chisel, saw,
and adze; the wood they marked,
the joints they cut: half-lap,
mortise, dovetail, and scarf,
locking roof-timbers tightly
in place: rafter, purlin,
tie-beam, and truss.

In parish churchyards they long
have lain, their voices silent,
their tongues turned to dust,
but some of their works yet remain,
carved from the resistant
grain of well-seasoned English
oak as strong and enduring
as the language they spoke.

Demolished Church

Where a church once stood upon hallowed ground,
Bare rubble, shattered glass and wood lie round,
And where once met the faithful and devout
Is a sign: Danger. Demolition Site. Keep Out.

Famine Relief

Something must be done, we say,
To help the starving children:

We'll send some money right away –
We've got enough to spare.

Such charity is christian
And shows that we really care.

Love Thine Enemy

With the fundamental Christian precept –
    Love Thine Enemy –
    I would wholeheartedly agree,

As long as my enemy will accept
    That he, just as wholeheartedly,
    Should also love me.

How old is? . . .

How old is grandma, grandpa?
    Well, she's older than her teeth
    And the same age as her tongue.

How old is grandpa, grandma?
    Well, to tell the honest truth,
    He still thinks he's twenty-one.

Guest–preacher, Good Friday
(Seion Chapel, Gorseinon, 2008)

He preaches by the chapel-gates,
The morning bleak and bare.
The faithful behind him shiver,
More used to pew or chair.
A raw gust sweeps the empty street
And lifts his thinning hair.

The few stray shoppers steal a glance
Then hurry on their way,
Too busy to stop and listen
To what he has to say
About a man called Jesus Christ
Who died for them this day.

Tony Paultyn

Terza Rima

For weeks on end, I've suffered pain –
This terza rima is a curse.
I've laboured long and hard, in vain,

To imitate this complex verse.
I've paced at midnight, back and fore,
But each new line appears far worse

Than the one I've written just before.
After sleepless nights, what have I done
But worn a hole in the bedroom floor.

My stumbling stanzas just won't run,
And seem so weak and airy-fairy
I wish, at times, I'd not begun.

This form's a snare to trap the unwary –
Unless you're Dante Allighieri.

Villanelles

How to write one of these is a job to explain,
With at least five tercets, as it were, in the frame,
Though the final stanza is a simple quatrain.

It was sung as a round with a complex refrain
And, although it's Italian, it has a French name.
How to write one of these is a job to explain.

A regular rhythm can be hard to maintain
(Yet many of the lines are exactly the same)
Though the final stanza is a simple quatrain.

You may play with the words and, perhaps, entertain,
But should stick all the time to the rules of the game.
How to write one of these is a job to explain.

I sincerely hope you'll have no wish to complain
If the feet of this poem seem slip-shod or lame,
Though the final stanza is a simple quatrain.

I'll apologise now, if you think it's a pain –
But I didn't invent it, so shan't take the blame.
How to write one of these is a job to explain,
Though the final stanza is a simple quatrain.

Al Capone

You had them all in your pocket –
the police chief, judge and mayor –
but no-one saw you pay the bribes,
for you, of course, weren't there.

You'd killed a call-girl in Brooklyn,
for keeping more than her share,
but no-one nailed you for the crime,
for you, of course, weren't there.

Some thought that Colosimo
should have taken far more care,
when iced inside his nightclub,
but you, of course, weren't there.

And sprawled among his roses,
lilies and maidenhair,
your rival, Dion O'Banion,
but you, of course, weren't there.

And slumped at the wheel of his Lincoln,
eyes fixed in a glassy stare,
your one-time buddy, Frankie Yale,
but you, of course, weren't there.

And seven men slain on Valentine's Day –
they didn't have a prayer –
lined up and shot against a wall,
but you, of course, weren't there.

And Giunta, Anselmi, Scalise –
each drunk and tied to a chair
beaten to pulp with a baseball bat,
but you, of course, weren't there.

And when you died, Saint Peter stood
at the top of the heavenly stair,
smiling beside an open door –
but you, of course, weren't there.

Al Capone's Wardrobe

Though he wore the best that money could buy –
The fedora hat, the hand-tailored suit,
The monogrammed shirt, the classy silk tie –
Beneath each stitch beat the blood of a brute.

Aphrodisiacs

Fresh sea-mussels, oysters and stout,
    Ambergris or caviar,
Swans' eggs mixed in a wedding-cake,
    Honey scooped from a jar –
All these I've tried, but must confide
    I've had no luck, so far.

The flesh of scarlet tomatoes
    (Love-apples ripe with lust),
The phallic horn of a rhino
    Ground finely into dust –
I've tried these, too, but in such charms
    Confess I cannot trust.

I have worn a slender leopard-bone
    Gilded upon my wrist,
And crushed-up hinges of scallop-shells
    Into a sensual grist –
But was there some ingredient
    That strangely I had missed?

So, in utter desperation,
    I'd no option but to try
A traditional aphrodisiac
    With the name of Spanish Fly –
Though, judging by the sad effect,
    I've often wondered why.

Baby Monkey

Soused, crab-raw, sour, curled up
Like a foetus in a jar,
Forehead pressed against smooth flat glass,
Knuckles blown with fine black hair,

You flinch, tiny hand clenched to mouth,
A look of anguish on your small tart face,
As if, imbrued with sourness,
You were retching in distaste.

A newborn drawn too soon from suckling,
Seeking a mother's warmth and care,
Crying in silence, your expression held
Forever in a grimace of despair –

Each feature faithfully preserved
From the moment you died.
All time and motion suspended
In a solution of formaldehyde.

For eternity, a specimen sealed
Behind glass, never to age or rot away,
Though the hair and skin of the hands
That pickled you have long ago decayed.

Lenin

You lie, preserved for posterity,
Embalmed in a mausoleum in Red Square,
Fingernails manicured, smooth wax skin, small
Mongol-eyes and wisps of neatly combed hair,
Kept at constant humidity and temperature
With a regular change of sterilized air.

Outside in the Russian winter,
Disposed of secretly in field or forest
Or the prison-camps of Siberia,
Are the bones of those who did not cooperate –
Poor peasant, rich farmer, who defied
The edicts of the Bolshevik state

And now lie buried in unmarked graves
Beneath fallen leaves or frozen grass,
While you, Vladimir Ilyich Lenin,
Revered by those who file slowly past,
Remain timeless, tight-lipped, unsmiling,
Sealed in a sarcophagus of bronze and glass.

Tattoo

Needled in black on an outstretched wrist,
A number filed on a lengthy list
Of those to be cleansed of lice and nits
At Treblinka, Belzec or Auschwitz.

Two Photographs
(Gulf War 1990–1991)

Burnt by napalm in the turret of a tank,
Caught half-out of the hatch in the act
Of escape, standing stiff and erect,
A young Iraqi soldier cooked
In his own juice, chargrilled in fat
Spat onto the hotplate of steel armour.

The pilot of the attack-helicopter
Who made this manikin of charred black ash,
Of melted flesh and welded hands stuck
To bare metal, at home on leave in the States
With wife and kids in a laughing summer garden
Stood by a barbecue searing raw steaks.

Chrysalis
(Gulf War 1990–1991)

The photograph framed what seemed the charred
Remains of a chrysalis – the imago half-emerged,
Urgent to escape the hatch in the pupal armour
That held it stuck, as if checked in the act
Of metamorphosis. Above it, the antennae bent
And withered by heat. Its forelimbs cauterized.
Its thorax scorched. Its abdomen still concealed
In the larval case. And yet, in its head, barely
Recognizable, through black sockets stared
The once-familiar features of a human face.

Verses for Hiroshima

Six miles high in a freezing sky
A B-29 droned slowly by.

Slender and white, her con-trail streamed.
The death she carried no-one dreamed.

All Clear wailed. The plane flew on.
Few would survive when she had gone –

The sky split in a blinding flash
Cremating all to atomic ash.

The fireball like a vengeance came
Scourging the earth with searing flame;

Spared not one leaf or blade of grass
And made stone start like melted glass.

From distant hill-tops, people gazed
Upon a city, flat, erased –

A desert of grey, smouldering dust
Where freak winds played in fitful gust.

On tracks through the wasteland, bowed in head,
Survivors trudged from the dying and dead.

"From where have you come?" They said, "That way."
"To where do you go?" They said, "This way."

Ghosting through the dust and smoke,
They trooped in silence. No-one spoke.

They held out arms, blistered and bare,
The raw burns weeping pink and rare.

Skin fell away in withered fold.
Flesh beneath lay clammy, cold.

In the chill of night, hundreds died
Seeking shelter, somewhere to hide,

While in days to come thousands would die
And those who witness wonder why –

No burn or sign of injury,
Their silent death a mystery.

Neutron, beta particle, gamma ray
Killed in a strange and secret way.

On life that stirred within the womb
Would fall the stillness of the tomb.

Returning to base, six miles high
The B-29 had long gone by.
Slender and white, her con-trail streamed.
The death she'd carried no-one dreamed.

When the A–bomb . . .

When the A-bomb fell from Enola Gay
Above Hiroshima that summer-day,
   A blind girl sensed an eerie flash
   As human beings turned to ash
One hundred miles away.

Johnny

"Johnny? Know him well! Hell of a boy, see.
(If it weren't the police, some girl or other.)
Surprised us all by joining the army –
Was never the type to take an order!
Made a smart lad of him, though . . .
Aye, called in last Christmas, home on leave . . ."

'Two o'clock they're bringing him. Down top-row.
Full military honours he'll receive.'

Song of the Broken Soldier

Leave me now
   Yet leave me
Beneath the open
    Sky,

And deck no cross
   Or solemn stone
With poppy
   When I die.

Lay me here
   Among these stones
Forget me
   When I'm dead,

For grasses wild
   Will fan my bones
And worms compose
   My bed.

And call not mine
   A glorious death
Nor laud me
   When I die,

Or off my stone
   The wind and rain
Shall wipe away
   The lie.

Battler Britton
(Second World War Comic Hero)

In my impressionable boyhood,
I declare, I was deeply smitten
By the daring war-time exploits
Of my hero, Battler Britton.

Doughty, death-defying, devil-may-care,
Utterly courageous, almost debonair,
Renowned for his feats of valour
By land or sea or air;

Known to all as the constant scourge
Of the Nazi war-machine:
The bane of the Luftwaffe,
The Wehrmacht, and the Kriegsmarine.

When Goering sent over his squadrons
After the fall of France,
The arrogant German pilots
Never gave us much of a chance –
But they didn't know that Battler and co.
Would lead them a merry dance.

I should like to quote an extract
From Battler's flying-log
That he kept beside a photograph
Of Biggles, his favourite dog.

(By the way, Battler's style of writing
Adds colour to the sense,
With the use of vivid description
And the present historic tense.)

'The alarm-bell goes – we grab our chutes,
Although we've hardly slept –
A raid approaching the Channel
We scramble to intercept.

'We gather speed for takeoff –
The ground goes whizzing by –
And with full boost from our engines,
We roar into the sky.

'As we cross the cliffs of Dover
In our Hurricanes and Spits,
We spot the enemy bombers
Shadowed by Messerschmitts.

'"Come on, chaps! Tally-ho!
Let's hit the blighters first!"
I get a Dornier in my sights
And give it a three-second burst.

'I bag a Heinkel one-eleven,
Then an Me. one-o-nine –
Tough luck, Fritz, you've had your chips,
For you, it's the end of the line."

'Suddenly, I spy a Focke-Wulf
Attacking out of the sun –
I spray his cockpit with cannon
And despatch another Hun.

'Down he goes in a ball of flame,
Crashing into the sea –
"Whacko, chaps!" I say, "that's enough for today;
Let's head back home for tea.

'"We've given Jerry a lesson
And put on a wizard show –
If he takes my advice, he'd better think twice,
If he wants another go."'

Although Battler became a famous ace
With a record number of kills,
His prowess as a fighter-pilot
Was but one of his many skills,

For he seemed the ultimate warrior,
An example to us all –
If High Command had a problem,
They knew the man to call.

Whether hunting for U-boats with asdic
In the cold Atlantic rain
Or holding a vital beachhead
In the Normandy campaign,

Fighting Rommel's Africa Corps
In the scorching desert sand
Or clearing Japs from the jungle
With a bren-gun in his hand,

Attacking Gestapo headquarters
In a daring commando-raid
Or blowing the tracks off a Panzer tank
With a single, well-aimed grenade

Tossed with just the right amount of spin
To break against a wicket –
A skill he learnt at Harrow
While captain of the cricket

(Meanwhile, the tank-crew stumble out,
Crying, "Raus! Schnell!" and "Donner und Blitzen!"
It must be that dirty Englander –
"Der Schweinhund, Battler Britton!") –

Battler was a superb all-rounder,
No matter the terrain;
I doubt if such a player
Could take the field again.

He was often asked to the Palace
For a medal-presentation,
And lauded by king George the sixth
As a credit to the nation.

"Congratulations, captain Britton,
I well remember your name;
By your glorious deeds of courage,
You truly deserve your fame."

Battler, clearly moved by these words,
Modestly bowed his head
And, gaining the king's permission to speak,
Opened his heart and said:

"That I have your majesty's approval
Is all I wish to know,
As I do my bounden duty
To fight against the foe.

"To win your approbation
Is more than I could ask;
I shall not falter, flounder, flag nor fail,
However hard the task.

"I do not seek for glory;
I do not wish for fame;
As long as people can say with pride
I played up and played the game."

"Well-spoken, captain Britton,
That really was first-rate;
With hearts so stalwart, staunch and strong,
We need not fear our fate."

He was welcomed next day by Churchill,
And greeted with pride and joy,
"Good to see you again, Battler,
How are you keeping, my boy?

"I'm ever so pleased you could spare the time
To drop in for some tea,
For I hear you've been rather busy of late
In winning your fifth VC,
The seventh bar to your DSO –
And yet another DFC!

"With your stirring acts of valour
Inspiring your men with pride,
It's lucky for us, Battler, my boy,
You're not on the other side!

"Without your brave example,
Who knows what we should do
I thank the Lord the Germans
Haven't got a man like you."

"You can count on me, prime minister,
To do my very best –
To serve my country in time of need
Unstintingly, without rest.

"I shall strive to do my duty
With honour, like a man,
From Norway to North Africa,
From Normandy to Japan.

"I'll fight the enemy anywhere –
Wherever the fiends might reach –
In the mountains, woods and fields,
In the streets or on the beach!"

"A splendid oration, Battler!
By damn, those words came out so well,
I might use them one day in Parliament
If you, h'm, promise not to tell."

"Most certainly: feel free, dear Winston,
To put them into one of your speeches –
As long as I can have the rest of that cake
And another dishful of peaches!"

But all good things, as they say, must end,
And when hostilities had to cease,
Battler, still infused with the urge to fight,
Felt bemused by the outbreak of peace

That came in the summer of '45
When the enemy was finally beaten –
Long after that slab of Dundee cake
And the tinful of peaches were eaten.

Yet I wonder what our hero did
When his fighting-days were over –
After he'd flown his last patrol
Above the cliffs of Dover.

Did he become the chief instructor
At Sandhurst, Dartmouth or Cranwell,
And a trusted adviser of Churchill
In his residence at Chartwell?

Or embrace the new, exciting command
Of a first-line fighter-station,
And win promotion up the ranks
Through skill and dedication?

Becoming, in time, an air-marshal
When, with medals in proud array,
He'd lay solemnly at a cenotaph
A wreath on Remembrance Day,

And after a long, distinguished career
Quietly choose to retire
To a cottage deep in the country
In some leafy English shire

And muse, perhaps, on scenes from his life
In dreamy contemplation,
Remembering the war-time scrambles
And the sense of fear and elation

When he and his fellow-pilots,
To cries of Yoicks! and Tally-ho!,
Showed those arrogant Nazi blighters
Exactly where to go;

So, with respect, I dedicate
The verses I have written
To the man by whom in my boyhood
I was so deeply smitten:
That most courageous warrior,
The indomitable Battler Britton.

Vietnam, Christmas Eve, ca. 1970

We have been ordered to relay
A message of peace and goodwill
To the Vietcong lines until
The stroke of midnight, Christmas Day,
But must in no way exceed the command,
For headquarters require
We resume artillery fire
In twenty-four hours, just as planned.

A.K. 47

No gun has sent to hell or heaven
More than the A.K. 47.

Equestrian Statue

He sits astride a martial steed
   Leading his last campaign,
A bronze hand held above his eyes,
   The other on the rein,
Staring across a city park
   Beneath the wintry rain.

He led a conquering army
   Into glory and to fame,
But now no-one remembers
   What was once a household name,
Or the victories that were gained
   In the battlesmoke and flame.

He knew the crack of the pistol,
   The flash of sabre and sword,
The horse-teams, guns and limbers
   On some dusty desert road
When he marched to tame the Afghan
   Or quell the Mahdi horde.

But his service to the Empire
   Is over now and done,
And long dead are the enemy
   Who fell to sword or gun,
And the glorious acts of valour
   Forgotten – every one.

Yet still, with martial mien, he stares,
   Leading his last campaign,
A bronze hand held above his eyes,
   The other on the rein,
As darkness falls across the park
   Beneath the wintry rain.

I wonder if a horse . . .

I wonder if a horse would ever say,
"I'm fed up of eating grass every day
Or filling my belly with oats and hay –
For all I care, you can take them away!"
The answer, I have no doubt, would be nay.

Abraham Lincoln

We think that we know you.
The dignified speech at Gettysburg.
Sober and staid as the stove-pipe hat
And dark frock-coat that you wore.

Yet how many know of your vigil
Each night in the telegraph-room?
Waiting for word of the fall of Richmond,
The end of the Civil War,

Or perceive, behind the relief,
The sadness such news might bring?
The fresh crop of widows, the empty farms,
The children who'd see their fathers no more.

And how can we but guess,
On looking at the bowed, silent head,
The sunken eyes, the lantern jaw,
The terrible weight that you bore?

Alan

Emotionally Disturbed,
the psychologist's words
typed beneath his name
in the school-records.

No problem, I thought.
A new teacher –
considerate, caring and kind,
I was sure we'd get on.

At times,
in the staffroom,
'How is Alan, today?'

'Oh, fine,' I'd reply.
'No problem. Why?'

Silence.
A knowing glance,
that's all,
as if to say,
just you wait.

Monday morning.
The secretary,
dinner-register in hand,
rising to go.

'Ah, I notice Alan
has some money, today.
He's on free meals,
as you know.
Has any gone missing?
Perhaps, you would ask?'

And I did.

And I did.

'Alan, the secretary said' –

7, 6,

'that you had some money,
this morning' –

5, 4,

(Head down.
Face darkening.)

3, 2,

'She wondered whether . . .'

'F___ off, you c___!
You f_____ bastard!
I always get the blame!'

Desks kicked over.
Chairs flung aside.
The door slammed.

After that,
it was never the same.

Each week, I'd go in.
Fearful.
Awaiting the detonation.

And it always came.

The New Boy

I'm afraid that the new boy, Headmaster,
Has got no respect for authority.
He always answers back, gets out of his seat,
Or interferes with someone or other.

He refuses to do what he's told
And acts like a law unto himself.
I'm beginning to lose control of the class,
For they feel that I cannot keep order.

Oh, come and sit down, and don't worry, Miss Jones,
I'm sure it's not as bad as you think.
In fact, look, I've just read this report
From the new Special Needs Adviser;

It came last week, h'm, with his old school-records.
In her opinion, he's a classic case
Of Attention Deficit Hyperactivity
And Oppositional Defiant Disorder.

There, now that you know what the problem is,
I'm sure you can find a solution.
With some suitable strategies in place,
I'm confident you can sort out the matter –

But don't forget, mind, my door is always open,
And if he's any trouble in the future
(And if I'm not busy) send him down with some work
And I'll put him outside in the corridor.

A Triolet on Schoolwork

Doing sums at his desk each day,
He'd look down, pretending to work.
He hoped Sir would keep well away,
Doing sums at his desk. Each day,
He'd yearn to hear the bell for play,
And seemed to do little but shirk,
Doing sums. At his desk each day,
He'd look down, pretending to work.

Snake

If milking a poisonous snake,
Take care, for safety's sake;
Hold its head tight because one bite
Might be your last mistake.

Cleopatra

"I'm sorry that I bit you,"
Said the asp to Cleopatra.
'Oh, don't worry about it,' she said,
'It doesn't really matter.'
Lying flat on the floor,
She didn't say any more.

Little Asp

"You must sibilate," said daddy asp, "like this,
And aspirate with heartfelt hate as you hiss."
'But dad,' said the little asp, 'I've got a lisp.'

Paruresis

If a man suffers from paruresis,
His psychological problem is this:
When stood by another, waiting to piss,
He feels far too shy and gives it a miss.

On Donating One's Body For Medical Research

Should anatomy students dissect me
In some chill pathology lab,
I'll have no more sense of the verb to be
Than a fish laid out on a slab.

41

Rhyming Dictionary

In the Penguin Rhyming Dictionary,
The only word listed to rhyme with corpse –
Evocative of a mortuary –
Is the northern seaside town of Cleethorpes.

Sound-words
(For 4 voices)

(All)   Listen carefully, for these lines abound
In words composed to echo sound:

(1)   Bludgeon, batter, bang and bash,
Clap, clout, clang and clash;

(2)   Sizzle, crackle, hiss and spit,
Creak, groan, crack and split;

(3)   Cuff, cudgel, thump and thwack,
Slam, slap, smite and smack;

(4)   Ring, jingle, chime and peal,
Squabble, scrabble, scream and squeal;

(All)   Yet the calls of quack, croak, bark and neigh,
Caw, squeak, bleat and bray,
Proclaim the point where we pass halfway –

(1)   With wail, weep, sob and sigh,
Shout, yell, laugh and cry;

(2)   Bubble, burble, blab and babble,
Giggle, gurgle, gab and gabble;

(3)   Biff, bam, wallop, wham,
Bomb, blitz, blast and blam;

(4)   Spill, gush, splatter, splash,
Howl, rage, hail and lash;

(All)   But beat, strike, bounce and bound,
Hit, hammer, punch and pound,
Finally nail this poem on sound.

Similes

(For 3 voices)

(1)   As rough as a brush,
As smooth as silk,
As bitter as bile,
As mild as milk.

(2)   As dry as a bone,
As wet as rain,
As dull as ditchwater,
As sharp as pain.

(3)   As fast as lightning,
As slow as a snail,
As soft as putty,
As hard as a nail.

(1)   As straight as a die,
As bent as a hook,
As white as a swan,
As black as a rook.

(2)   As round as a ball,
As square as a box,
As weak as a baby,
As strong as an ox.

(3)   As small as a mouse,
As big as a whale,
As calm as a breeze,
As wild as a gale.

(1)   As stale as old bread,
As fresh as new paint,
As corrupt as a devil,
As pure as a saint.

(2)   As light as a feather,
As heavy as lead,
As frisky as a kitten,
As still as the dead.

(3)   As cold as ice,
As warm as toast,
As dark as a tomb,
As pale as a ghost.

(All)   But now our similes
Must draw to a close –
As sour as vinegar,
As sweet as a rose –
But which ones are true
Nobody knows.

Opposites
(For 4 voices)

(All)   The opposite of day is night;
       The opposite of young is old;
    The opposite of black is white;
       The opposite of hot is cold.

(1)   Of out is in;
         Of up is down;
      Of fat is thin;
         Of smile is frown.

(2)   Of high is low;
         Of love is hate;
      Of fast is slow;
         Of early, late.

(3)   Of weak is strong;
         Of bless is curse;
      Of right is wrong;
         Of better, worse.

(4)   Of front is back;
         Of east is west;
      Of tight is slack;
         Of work is rest.

(All)   The opposite of smooth is rough;
       The opposite of tame is wild;
    The opposite of tender, tough;
       The opposite of bitter, mild.

(1)   Of boon is bane;
         Of faith is doubt;
      Of pleasure, pain;
         Of whisper, shout.

(2)   Of big is small;
         Of push is pull;
      Of short is tall;
         Of empty, full.

(3)　　　Of laugh is cry;
　　　　　Of give is take;
　　　Of wet is dry;
　　　　　Of balm is ache.

(4)　　　Of good is bad;
　　　　　Of truth is lies;
　　　Of happy, sad;
　　　　　Of foolish, wise.

(All)　The opposite of war is peace;
　　　　The opposite of foe is friend;
　　　The opposite of begin is cease,
　　　　And the opposite of start is end.

Collective Nouns
(For 3 voices)

(1)   A labour of moles,
        A building of rooks,
        A colander of holes,
        A library of books.

(2)   A flotilla of boats,
        A division of police,
        A tribe of goats,
        A gaggle of geese.

(3)   A skein of silk,
        A swarm of bees,
        A churn of milk,
        A round of cheese.

(1)   A stack of boxes,
        A sheaf of arrows,
        A skulk of foxes,
        A host of sparrows.

(2)   A plague of rats,
        A herd of hogs,
        A clowder of cats,
        A pack of dogs.

(3)   A baren of mules,
        A bag of bolts,
        A box of tools,
        A rag of colts.

(1)   A pulpit of preachers,
        A bevy of quails,
        A staff of teachers,
        A school of whales.

(2)   A heap of leaves,
        A down of hares,
        A gang of thieves,
        A sloth of bears.

(3)   A stand of plovers,
        A fleet of cars,
        A sighing of lovers,
        A galaxy of stars.

(All)   But a circus of clowns
        Must bring to an end
        The collective nouns
        That we have penned –
        With a culture of yeast,
        A wisp of snipe,
        And, last, but not least,
        A load of tripe.

Senghenydd
(October 14, 1913)

I open the Book of Remembrance.
I turn each page with reverential care,
Fingers muffled by soft, white gloves,
Insulated from grief,
From the entries neatly written
In alphabetical order:
Davies, Evans, Jones ...
I feel nothing for the names,
By distance and by time estranged
From the noise and filth of the pit,
From that Autumn day –
The blast ripping up through the downcast,
The pithead-whistle shrill with steam,
The rescue-teams, the policemen,
The reporters up from Cardiff,
And relatives at the pit-gates
Flocking for news, before returning
Distraught, to street after street
Of curtains drawn in mourning.

I see one in her kitchen clutching an apron,
Widowed eyes blind with grief,
Yearning to hear, again, the end of a shift,
The sound of boots on the street,
The click of the latch,
The water hot on the hob
Waiting to wash the collier's back,
Muscled and warm,
She never again would touch.
The door is shut, the latch unlifted,
The tin bath vacant on its nail
In the backyard,
For he lies cold on the floor of the smithy,
Amid row upon row of men and boys
Killed two thousand feet below.

Unknown to her, the terrified calls
Of father and son,
The floundering bodies,
The choking gasps,
The searing heat of the firedamp
Flaring in a wall of flame,
The crackling timbers,
The acrid smoke,
Pit-ponies pitched over in harness,
Scorched from fetlock to mane,
And later, by the light
Of rescue-lamps,
In heading and stall,
The dead face-down in the afterdamp.

No-one knew the cause of the blast
That blew so many through the dark,
But here, grief subdued, the room
Sombre and still, I am loth to stay,
To touch on leaves the names
Of ghosts brought long ago to bank.
I shut the book. Take off the gloves.
Reverently, they are returned
Like exhibits to a hardwood cabinet,
The lid closed and dutifully locked.
The pit, they said, was a bad one for dust
And gas. I turn to leave, quiet
With respect, and see, beside the book,
The gloves – the pair of soft, white gloves –
Laid out neatly beneath the glass.

The Announcer
(For C., 1989)

Listening to the local radio
While driving each morning to work,
Men fell in love with your warm, velvet voice
And hung on the words that you spoke.

And they sent you flowers and fan-mail
And proposals over the phone
And ardent appeals for a photograph,
For your face was, as yet, unknown,

Until the day you were recognised
And, despite your beautiful voice,
Were considered so plain in features
That men wouldn't look at you twice.

Feeling rejected, you stayed off work,
Unable to cope with the pain,
Spending long days alone in your flat,
Not wanting to broadcast again.

And the men who had said they loved you
And had wanted you for their wife
Heard one night as they drove home from work
You'd been driven to take your life.

On the Suicide of Alan Turing

A shy epicene,
He had died unseen,
As if shamed by some sexual stigma.

He'd been called unclean
And his thoughts obscene,
But his genius had broken Enigma.

Visit

She lies, curled-up, in a hospital bed,
The sheets drawn tight around her head,

Turned to the wall, wishing not to be seen,
Willing the nurse to bring back the screen.

Meaningless, the tinsel, the lights on the tree
That seem to mock in irony

This girl in trauma at the end of the ward,
Withdrawn for days without gesture or word,

As if in despair she could not hide
The shame of failing her suicide.

Birth

The infant delivered, two electrodes
Monitoring heartbeat were unclipped
From its scalp. The stainless tight
Teeth of two forceps to the umbilical
Cord were clamped. Its mouth inspected –
Palate uncleft. Length and weight recorded.
Reflexes checked. Sexed and tagged
With time, date of birth and identity.
Its existence already quantified.
Defined by data wherever it goes – long
After the counting of fingers and toes.

Why? . . .

Why is it that women show pique
　　Or feel such acute distress?
When they see another look chic
　　In an identical dress.

Metal Rule

Graduated. Definitive. Precise.
I am rigid and correct.
I bring order to your life.

Do not ever misuse me.
I have a hard, straight edge
That can cut like a knife.

Look only to me for guidance.
I am always in the right.
I am your ruler: I am your wife.

The Widow

She found that the dust of her late husband –
Too lazy and shiftless to shake a leg –
If put to work in a kitchen timer,
Could be quite useful when boiling an egg.

Public Statue

Heads back, raucous, beaks gaping wide,
Citified seagulls screech and chide,
While he, unmoving, stiff with pride,
Decorous, staid and dignified,
Takes their stridency in his stride
And seems in no way mortified
On feeling something slimy slide
Down his face from a bird's backside.

Stuck in the Outside Loo

"Open the door!" yelled the old man,
"I've dropped my false teeth down the pan!
The bulb has gone – there ain't no light!
I can't stay shut in 'ere all night!"
Incensed with rage, he kicked at the seat,
Tripped on the braces round his feet,
Then stumbling with a cry of pain,
He blindly grabbed and clanked the chain –
Swept onward in the foaming rush,
His dentures vanished down the flush.
Next day, at play in the sewer beneath,
A frisky young rat found the set of teeth;
Now all his girlfriends think he's ace –
A sparkling smile across his face.

Overheard in Dagenham
(January, 1968)

"Yeh, but 'e wouldn't be so 'appy if
'e knew where 'e was going," she replied –
drily powdered and furred, with a pink face
at the bus-stop. She took a seat inside.

"I 'ad to take a day off work. Cain't seem
to get a lie-in anytime, nah, what
with the old man off sick, an' 'im coughing
most ev'ry morning . . . H'm, 'twould do a lot

"o' good, but 'e cain't give it up, can 'e?
An' to think this little dog 'ere ain't 'ad
a fag all 'is life . . . Yeh, 'e do look cute,
don't 'e, but 'e's got to go. Feel bit sad

"'bout it, sometimes. Still, it'll be a change
what with no more scraps all over the floor
an' clearing up after 'im – cain't control
'is motions prop'ly. Nah, not anymore.

"An' there's all that trouble with the bleeding
licence ev'ry year, an' 'is box to keep
clean, so we're 'aving 'im put dahn. They say
it's painless, you know, an', 'sides, it's cheap,

"ev'rything considered. We've 'ad 'im ten
years, nah – an' always looked after 'im well,
mind you! But that's gorn and past – 'e's gotten
too old for fun. Ev' since 'e got took ill,

"'e ain't been the same. An' 'e used to be
such a lively little thing. But that's fate,
I s'pose. Any'ow, must go! 'ere's my stop.
I'm early – so 'e won't 'ave long to wait."

Yellow

Yellow as a bowl
Of golden custard,
As Cheddar cheese
Or English mustard.

Yellow as a buttercup
Held to the chin,
And the petals of primrose,
Broom, and whin.

Yellow as a field
Of ripening corn.
Yellow as boxwood
Freshly sawn.

Yellow as the rind
Of a honeydew melon,
And the citric skin
Of a sour lemon.

Yellow as the gape
Of a swallow chick,
And sunlit straw
In a farmer's rick.

Yellow as egg yolk,
Yellow as ghee,
Yellow as pollen
On the leg of a bee –
And yellow as catkins,
The Spring-time catkins,
The trembling catkins
On a hazel tree.

Rose

The Rose of Lancaster was red as blood;
    The Rose of York was white as snow;
From the blood and bone of Bosworth Field,
    The hybrid Tudor Rose would grow.

White

White as spume
That breakers fling,
A feather dropped
From a seagull's wing.

White as a snowdrop
Chilled by ice,
White as the petals
Of edelweiss.

White as milk
In a brimming pail,
White as silk
In a bridal veil –

And white as the throat,
The swelling throat,
The sweet trilling throat
Of a nightingale.

Red

Red as petals
Of poppy or phlox,
Red as paint
On a pillar-box.

Red as the skin
Of a holly-berry,
As a ripe bell-pepper,
Plum or cherry.

Red as blood
From a bleeding nose,
Red as varnish
On a woman's toes –

And red as the blush,
The voluptuous blush,
The soft, velvet blush
Of a garden rose.

Limerick

A sensitive chap called Egan
Decided to live as a Vegan –
    Lots of Marmite on toast
    And crunchy nut-roast
With beansprouts was all he would feed on.

Limerick

A parrot called Polly ap Price
Got banned from Twickenham twice –
    He'd flown through the crowd
    While squawking aloud,
"Twll du bob blydi Sais!"

Limerick

A barmy young chap called East
Abstained from the eating of yeast –
    He thought even mould
    Had a right to grow old
And its soul rise to God when deceased.

Titanic

In the cold, dark depths on the ocean-bed,
No vestige remains of a man long dead,
Except two shoes side by side in the sand,
Laced by the fingers of a vanished hand.

Epitaph on a Taxidermist

He who would stuff the pheasant, stoat, and hare,
The hunted fox or rabbit choked by snare,
Stiffens in death with the same glassy stare.

Epitaph on a Carpenter

He who could lock a joint
Tight with tenon and mortise,
Lies with tendon and joint
Locked tight in rigor mortis.

Deathly Synonyms

If you've ridden on your last roundup,
Or crossed the great divide;
If you lodge in the happy hunting ground,
Or with Abraham abide;
If you've joined the silent majority,
Or passed to the other side,
Then you must have kicked the bucket,
Or, in other words, have died.

Senility

Sitting on a chair in a state of inertia,
Completely lacking any sense of adventure,
Becoming more wrinkled and withered in feature
And but dimly aware of senile dementia,
I shall die, perhaps, from a cardiac seizure,
And be consigned, at length, to an undertaker
To lie in a box in a funeral parlour
As cold and dark as a refrigerator
(But without any risk of hypothermia),
Destined for the cheaper of two crematoria
Where, dead on time and in accord with procedure,
My weight on a shoulder of each well-paid bearer,
I'll be borne up the aisle with solemn composure
To be placed on a dais in front of the altar;
And after a service led by a minister
(Two hymns and a sermon about the hereafter
With familial anecdotes tinged with nostalgia
And a pop-song, no doubt, relayed through a speaker),
I shall slowly descend in an elevator
To await my turn at the incinerator.

On a First-floor Landing

An elderly widow
With snow-white hair,
Sitting in her flat
Alone in a chair,
Looks at the window
With a vacant stare,
Her door half-open
But she unaware
That the eyes of a stranger
Watch her there.

Shroud

You might find many pick-pockets
In a crowd,
But you won't find any pockets
In a shroud.

Grave

From the cold of the grave I shall not wake
   Nor ever again shall sunlight see,
Though the blow of a spade my bones might break
     In delving a bed
     For one new-dead
Whose time has come to lie with me.

Al Capone on Alcatraz

Locked up in sol, went off his sconce, when called
Scarface, not cool Alphonse;
"I was big, once – not a ponce!"
Silence, the bare walls' response.

My Dad

Moody, might have a paddy. In high jinks,
Still thinks he's a laddie.
Will moo and boo, a baddy.
Sometimes mad, he's my daddy.

Death of Alan Turing

Distraught, his own destroyer, he'd bitten
His last apple, bitter.
Stained by sexual stigma,
Disowned, died in dishonour.

Dylan on a Chair, Swansea Marina (1)

Speaking to the spellbound air, Dylan stops,
Then slowly turns to stare,
Seeming in some way aware
A stranger he knew stood there.

Dylan on a Chair, Swansea Marina (2)

Sculptured to his natural size, he stirs,
As if starting to rise,
Turning half-round, in surprise,
To stare with his sightless eyes.

On Dylan's Grave

Where grass upon his grave has grown, and winds
Of bleak winters have blown,
Flesh has been stripped from the bone
But words still sing through the stone.

Herpetologist

A hapless herpetologist once clasped
An asp within his fist;
Riled by this, the reptile hissed,
Whipped round fast and bit his wrist.

Ludwig Mond
(19th Century Industrial Chemist)

Imagine a magic wand. A wizard.
Hand raised. A black hat donned.
Spells to make chemicals bond.
A master-mind: Mister Mond!

Alan Turing

A stickler most painstaking, his bright brain
Brilliant at code-breaking,
Sifting and deciphering.
In talent towering – Turing.

On the Statue of Aneurin Bevan (1897–1960), Queen Street, Cardiff

Composed, as if poised to reply, he stands
Statesman-like, head held high,
Smartly dressed in suit and tie –
The ex-miner men call Nye.

Aneurin Bevan, Politician

With rapier-tongued repartee, he debunked
While debating with glee
And, through artful oratory,
Made our fee-fraught healthcare free.

On the Statue of John Batchelor (1820–1883), The Hayes, Cardiff

The sculpture of John Batchelor that stands
Staid and proud in posture,
Though streaked with birds' excreta,
Stays stately still in stature.

On the Bronze Statue of a Victorian Dignitary

Befouled by sea-fowls' effluence, demeaned
In his munificence,
His cast, costly eminence
An avian convenience.

Pylons

Lofty and aloof with pride, strictly drilled,
Long lines of pylons stride,
Highly strung, electrified,
Straight across the countryside.

Rapist

The rapist saw a therapist. "From lust,"
She said, "you must desist.
Sex so lewd and rude resist."
'Yes,' he hissed, 'I get the gist!'

Scott's Party Nears the South Pole

In the distance, barely visible,
A small, dark dot was discernible,
Specking the top of an icy knoll;

Then their frost-bitten feet seemed to drag
And their sledge-hauling shoulders to sag,
As if the sight had sickened their soul,

For they knew it was Amundsen's flag
And they'd failed to be first to the Pole.

Scott Sights the South Pole

A dark Norse flag, stark, austere, Scott's party
Spied as the Pole drew near;
Each man, chastened, loth to cheer,
Heaved on still the heavy gear.

Scott, Beaten to the South Pole

Forestalled at the Pole, sorely stressed, Scott's men,
Hope scotched, just longed to rest;
Looked exhausted, lacking zest,
Piqued they'd lost the polar quest.

Scott's Party Leaves the Pole

Having failed, feeling subdued, on their tracks
Trekked back in sombre mood;
Left to silent solitude
That desolate latitude.

On the Death of Edgar Evans
(A Member of Scott's Polar Party, 1912)

Brain-injured, wearied by labour,
He'd heave the sledge no further,
But hang behind and hinder
And, wayward, start to wander.

At night, silently in slumber,
He slipped into a coma.
Beneath the Beardmore Glacier
Lies his icy sepulchre.

On the Marble Bust of Edgar Evans
(A Member of Scott's Polar Party, 1912)

An ex-polar explorer, cleanly carved
In cold, white Carrara,
Still warmed, through skill of sculptor,
By scarf and balaclava.

Edgar Evans
(1876–1912)

The memorial plaque in Rhossili church
And the carved bust in Swansea museum
Are both made of smooth Italian marble
As white and cold as the ice of the Pole.

The Discovery of Scott's Tent

One man saw a canvas vent – scraped the snow
Aside and cried, "Scott's tent!"
Still, as if sleeping, silent,
Three men the world would lament.

The Finding of Scott's Remains
(November 12, 1912)

With no sign of Scott, a relief party was sent
But nothing in that white waste could any man see
Until one spied what seemed to be a canvas vent
Half-buried in a drift and, beneath it, a tent.
They scraped away the ice and snow frantically,
Then paused, fearing what the ominous stillness meant.
One drew the flap, peered in, but perceived no movement –
Only sleeping-bags with the gaunt figures of three
Men: Wilson, Scott and Bowers, lying adjacent
To each other, frozen, dignified and silent,
As if they had all foreknown what their fate would be.
From their thin, scurvied features, it was evident
They had died of hunger, cold and malnourishment,
With all rations gone, save for scant sugar and tea.
Slowly, they struck Scott's last camp with grave deportment,
Folding it over the dead and their equipment;
Read out a few words with heads bowed in dignity,
Then, unable to dig through earth for interment,
Raised a cairn of snow with skis crossed for their monument

Rhino

When we watched it browse the African bush –
Stripping shrivelled leaves in time of drought
Or grazing after rain when grass grew lush –
Its survival seemed never in doubt,
For its body moved like a battletank
Clad in plates of thick black leather
Shielding neck and shoulder, back and flank
In a tight, impregnable armour.
But today we find it felled in the sun
By a high velocity rifle-shot,
Cut down in ambush by a poacher's gun,
A bloated carcase left to rot.
And its hide, once proof against spine or thorn,
No more a defence than the hacked-off horn.

To a Rhino Poacher

The phallic horn of the rhino
   (Now increasingly rare),
Has as much medicinal value
   As a spike of matted hair.

It resembles in chemical structure
   The hoof of a farmyard-cow.
It can neither alleviate fever
   Nor with sexual zest endow;

Therefore, let the rhino wander
   The land where it was born,
Not with machine-gun murder
   And hack away its horn.

Hedgehog

With moist, black nose and spire snout,
for slugs and snails you venture out;
push through brambles or dewy grass
that wet your prickles as you pass;
and then, night gone, to bed you creep
and curl beneath dead leaves in sleep.

Victim of a passing car,
body squashed into chipping and tar,
a thorny pelt ironed flat on the road,
a bit of trash discarded, ignored,
brown as a pat of dung
caked and dry in the sun.

Aspects of an Elephant

Each of its great limbs
Stands smooth and round
As the bole of a beech.

Its long trunk swings
Like a length
Of old fire-hose.

And its ears,
Rivered with veins,
Flap like huge, brown maps
Of Africa.

Blackbird

I cannot hear the blackbird sing:
The cat next door has killed the Spring.

The Crash, 1997
(A prose-poem)

(After the crash, the paparazzi offered to release a photograph of
princess Diana mortally injured in the back of a car – if a payment
of £300,000 was made.)

In addition, the following exclusive
images were on offer to the trade:

the head of John the Baptist
on a silver salver laid;

the delicate skin of a Jew
for a Nazi lampshade flayed;

the death of Thomas à Becket,
slain by a sword as he prayed;

or Christ impaled on a cross,
the wounds in his hands displayed –

as long as a deal could be struck
and cash on-the-nail be paid.

Incident in Berlin, 1962
(In memory of Peter Fechter, 18 years of age)

On the front page of a newspaper
a photograph of a man
slumped on a concrete wall,
an East German bullet in his back,
crying softly in pain.

No-one dares go near,
but a press-photographer
from a safe distance
carefully aims his telephoto lens
and takes another shot.

The Two Skeletons

Said Skeleton Two to Skeleton One,
"A bed in the churchyard isn't much fun."

"Aye," said Skeleton One to Skeleton Two –
"If you're laid-out beside a griper like you."

"I've been mouldering here," said Two, "for years.
There's earth in the holes where used to be ears,
A bald bone crown where used to be hair
No wonder I feel such utter despair.
My two white eyes into bony sockets
Have sunk like billiard-balls into their pockets;
My bodily functions have long ago stopped;
My teeth have come loose; my jaw-bone has dropped.
To loam have turned lips that used to be kissed,
And scattered like tesserae the bones of my wrist.
I can't hear the rain; I can't see the sun . . ."

"Oh, stop complaining," said Skeleton One.
"My body, too, is turning to dust;
The screws of my coffin are eaten with rust,
But I don't grizzle and bemoan my plight;
Just give it a rest you've been carping all night."

For a while, there was silence. They lay there so stiff,
Not talking, like lovers just after a tiff,
Till Skeleton Two, with a sense of unease,
Whispered softly to One in an effort to please,
"The cap has gone missing from one of my knees."
Wrongly assuming a sense of rapport,
It carried on moaning just like before:
"This place is unhealthy. It's crawling with germs.
And to make matters worse, I think I've got worms.
The rib-cage is hollow where once beat a heart . . ."

"Oh, not again!" cried One. "Now don't bloody start!
My bowels have gone – I can't even fart!"

"Trust you to be rude," said Two. "You think you're dead smart,
But you're common as muck, and that's the truth.
You've got no breeding. You're coarse and uncouth.
Whenever you speak, you lower the tone.

Oh, deprived of culture, I feel so alone,
Stuck next to you as still as a stone –
Small wonder I'm driven to whimper and moan.
The ground feels so hard my pelvis is numb –
It's such a discomfort not having a bum.
My bones like old sticks are brown with decay;
My mouth cannot shut – it's filling with clay . . ."

"Then how come," said the other, "you've got so much to say?"

"Don't be sarcastic and try to be snide!"
Cried Two, in a pique, to the bones by its side.
"Although I might seem a bore and a pain,
And rather inclined to whinge and complain,
No matter what you think, with all said and done,
A bed in the churchyard isn't much fun.
It's damp, depressing, dreary and dull . . ."

"Aye, just like you," muttered Skeleton One.

"I heard that remark," said Skeleton Two,
"Just lie there and scoff – that's all you can do –
But sometimes I feel bored out of my skull!"

"Oh, for pete's sake, be quiet," said Skeleton One.
"All I hear every day are grumbles and groans.
Can't you stop whining – you bag of old bones!
I wish they'd buried you an extra foot deep.
Now give me some peace and go back to sleep."

So bickered two skeletons in the grave where they lay.
What one would affirm the other'd gainsay
And, as far as I know, they're still at it today.

Fly

As a fly, I do not think it rude
Or my table-manners somewhat crude,
To vomit on your wasted food,

And when the puke is soft and runny,
To suck it back into my tummy
(A taste, I swear, like that of honey).

You might deem your manners better than mine
When you put on airs and sit down to dine
Or finish your meal with cheese and wine,

And believe, perhaps, when you choose to eat,
That peaches and cream is a gorgeous treat
But I find faeces far more sweet.

You can keep your salad with mayonnaise,
Your chicken chow mein or spaghetti Bolognese
Or apple-pie with crème Anglaise,

Your tasty Cheddar or smoked applewood,
Your sirloin roast with Yorkshire pud,
For none of these is half as good

As a hearty helping of horse-manure
Or something floating down a sewer
With the lovely fragrance of ordure.

(I regard myself as a connoisseur
With the palate of an epicure,
When it comes to items in a sewer.)

I cannot help but take a peek
At sewage with a wholesome reek,
Untreated for at least a week.

To you, a blockage in a sink,
Or a septic tank, have a horrid stink,
But, to me, such things are meat and drink.

I love foul drains and effluent,
And you'll often find that I frequent
A farmyard for its excrement –

On stuff that cattle defecate,
With fellow-flies I'll congregate
In a sudden urge to procreate.

(It seems the fragrance might induce –
As if we needed some excuse –
The strong desire to reproduce.)

On dung of any shape or form,
Especially if it's soft and warm,
I'll find a mate within the swarm

And, after frenzied copulation,
Fertilized by impregnation,
Secrete my eggs for incubation –

Perhaps on the corpse of a homicide,
Its jaw hung open, gaping wide,
Hidden by scrub in the countryside.

I'll lay my eggs on foetid skin –
Inside the mouth, beneath the chin,
Or eyelids where it's moist and thin –

Then fly away, my business done,
And hope my offspring, one by one,
Will hatch beneath the warming sun.

The grubs may pierce eye or lip
And softened flesh will slowly strip
Clean from toe to finger-tip.

Listen, you might hear them rustle,
As they worm through fat and gristle,
Eating down into the muscle

And, as if by liquefaction,
On the site of putrefaction,
Through ingestion and excretion,

Consume the flesh that lies within
Till all the corpse is shrunk and thin,
And nothing's left but bone and skin.

(By the way, I pride myself on dining well
In direct proportion to the smell
A corpse gives off as it starts to swell.)

In fact, from things that decompose –
And make mere humans hold their nose –
The scent is lovelier than a rose.

I deem irresistible, I have to say,
Particularly on a sunny day,
The alluring odour of decay.

From over a mile in the summer heat,
I can trace the smell of rotting meat
And taste, when I land, with pads in my feet.

I may home like a devil drawn by sin
On juicy titbits found within
The contents of your rubbish-bin,

But for most of your food I care not a scrap –
For your curry and chips or burger in a bap,
For I much prefer to dine on crap.

Although you might find my lifestyle iffy,
With the pleasure I take in all things niffy
(So strong, at times, they make *me* squiffy)

There is one proud fact you should not ignore:
In my time on earth, I have killed far more
Than you have slain through your acts of war.

I have long been a vector of deadly disease
(Along with mosquitoes, lice and fleas)
Spreading filth and germs wherever I please,

But do not condemn the things that I do,
Such as feeding on garbage, sewage or poo,
For in some respects, I'm superior to you.

I perform many feats that you wouldn't dare –
I can fly upside-down or hover mid-air
(And both with consummate skill and flair).

I may land on a ceiling or walk up a wall
Without any fear of height, at all,
Or the slightest concern that I might fall.

I've delicate wings and feelers, too,
Six slender legs, while you have two,
And must with stunted limbs, called arms, make do.

I have lived on this earth (or so it appears,
From the fossilized remains of my forebears)
For more than three hundred million years –
Long, long before the age of the dinosaurs.

For how long, may I ask, have you?

Housefly

I enter your house and take a peep;
I hear you breathing slow and deep,
Slumped in an armchair, fast asleep.

You seem so harmless, dozing there,
With ample girth and thinning hair –
Yet something tells me to beware

For, despite the care I undertake
To minimize the sound I make,
You hear me buzzing, and awake.

Rubbing your eyes, you mutter, 'Drat!'
And, although you look unfit and fat,
You leap to your feet and bellow, 'Scat!'

I fly for refuge into the kitchen,
And land on a window, feelers twitching,
Till you rush in, as if you are itching

(A rolled-up tabloid tight in your grasp,
Incensed by my toilet with its flecks of frass)
To splat my body against the glass.

But I'm too fast for you to hit,
And soon have vanished, lickety-split –
While you, outsmarted, feel a twit.

When you spy me grooming on the bread,
Your smouldering anger starts to spread,
And dewlap, jowls and face go red.

As I stroke my wings and fuss and preen,
You utter something quite obscene,
And call me loathsome and unclean.

You loom above me like a behemoth,
Raising your fist in righteous wrath,
Then bang it down on the tablecloth.

You smash the teapot, spill the tea,
And rattle all the crockery,
In a vain attempt to murder me.

I see a saucer, then a plate,
Launched into orbit by your hate,
Against the wall disintegrate.

Fuming in anger, you grab a broom
And chase me madly through the room,
The look on your face presaging doom.

You climb ungainly onto the table
To reach as far as you are able,
Yet your posture seems a mite unstable

And, as you make a desperate lunge
(My delicate body to expunge),
Your footing slips, and down you plunge.

Landing with a fearful smack,
You lie flat-out upon your back,
Your outstretched arm grown limp and slack.

Then, rising menacingly from the floor,
Disgruntled, stiff, and rather sore,
You slyly shut the kitchen-door.

You turn to the cupboard beneath the sink;
I hear a faint metallic clink,
Though what it is I dread to think,

But all too soon I understand
The evil deed that you have planned,
When I see an aerosol in your hand.

You finger the button on the tin;
Your smile becomes a twisted grin –
It's clear you mean to do me in.

I realize I'm in a scrape,
And fly behind the window-drape
In a frantic effort to escape.

Although I flee, I cannot hide,
And feel distraught and terrified
As you spray me with insecticide.

Desperately, I dive and twist,
Hoping that you might have missed,
Then meet a cold and clinging mist.

Paralysed by the stinging cloud,
My abdomen droops, my head is bowed –
The vapour wraps me like a shroud.

Out of control, I have to ditch;
My blind eyes burn; my feelers itch;
Flat on the floor, I start to twitch.

I move my wings but cannot fly.
However long or hard I try,
I fail to stir from where I lie –

Not seeing my human enemy,
In his final act of infamy,
With brush and pan, swoop down to attack;

Sweep me swiftly off my back,
And, heedless of the irony,
Dump me in a rubbish-sack.

Housefly's Complaint

I am a forthright, friendly fly,
And cannot help but wonder why
You'd like so much to see me die.

That I have a love of human sewage
As much as rotten fish or cabbage
Thrown away in your household garbage

Is something that I must confess,
Yet the fact I thrive is due no less
To your fondness for uncleanliness;

Thus, if I should land on doggy-poo
Or the fragrant bowl of an unclean loo,
Don't show disgust at what I do
When the blame, perhaps, might lie with you.

Ladybird

Please, don't pick me up
And give me a squeeze,
Or thin green blood
Might leak from my knees.

Flea

In excess
Of one hundred Gs,
A flea will leap off its knees,

For the stress
Of this awesome feat
Would break its delicate feet.

A flea

A man compressed
To a flea
Could spring
The tallest tree.

Knife

I can chop and dice, stab, slit, slash and slice,
And have done some things that weren't very nice
Like cutting the tails off the three blind mice;
So use me with care – I shan't tell you twice.

Flies on a Car's Headlights

I stood
by a graveyard this night,
hands on
bars mellowing touch. Stood
and saw
or, perhaps, noticed. I
did not
know what it was that I
was drawn
to or, rather, why it
was it
was to that I turned. Yet
I did
turn, to a car's lamps – grizz-
-led lines
across glass – for I wond-
-ered what
could mist or mizzle the
glass. Turned
and stroked, on peering, with
my nail,
a myriad tiny flies,
like an
army flung and poised there,
tacked by
blood and wing. A graveyard
on cold
glass, as it were, stirred by
my fing-
-er's nail. A pitiful
gesture
I could not to the oth-
-er dead
make. Though that was irrel-
-evant,
for I could do nothing
for them.
Moist. Stirring. Throbbing like
a light,
soft drum under my nail.

The Shadow

An electric light,
A chair beneath
And, beneath that,
Motionless, black,
Its image.

It would have been hard
To predict
The exactness of the shape –
To have anticipated
The stark limits
That the chair cast:
They had already been defined
And seemed able
Neither to move nor change.

Laid-out
To a precise logic.
Staining the floor
With a sawed dark pool
Of shadow.

Tulips

Slender

Green and still

Tulips drink

From a glass vase

Unconscious

Of the clearness

Filling their veins

Delicately

Silently

Sluicing each tall

Sliced stem

And flowerhead.

Pendulum

Before the long,
Slow pendulum
Of the prison-clock
Could return
Along the arc
Of its swing –
To where, precisely,
But a moment before,
Its sweep had begun –
The trap dropped,
A neck cracked,
And a dead man swung.

If you walk . . .

If you walk on the lawn of Wandsworth jail,
Be careful where you tread;
Beneath the grass are the graves of those
Whose feet to the gallows led.

How many dead? . . .

How many dead,
Guiltless of crime,
Burned in a bed
Of hangman's lime?

Electric Chair

On first seeing the state-execution
Of a prisoner by electrocution,
One might find revolting the excretion
Of bodily waste with a sudden hiss,
And be shocked by the smell of shit and piss,
But one, in time, becomes inured to this.

The Electrocutors

We'll make you jolt from head to feet,
Your heart race on or cease to beat,
And flesh start burning in the heat.

Your body will convulse with shock,
Your eyeballs bulge, your jawbone lock,
And knees and elbows quake and knock.

But if the treatment is in vain
And life still stirs within your brain,
We'll switch the current on again.

The Appointment
(A prose-poem)

Sit down, make yourself comfortable. Try to relax –
the treatment won't take long. The arm-rests? – Yes, covered
in rubber – much warmer than bare metal, isn't it?

Now, it's important we have you safe and secure,
so let me just slip this strap around your ankles and ease
off your slippers. Keep your feet together – rest them on
the plate. That's it! Now for your wrists. There, how's
that? Not too tight, I hope.

The dryer? Oh, the helmet – yes, it does *look* like
a dryer, doesn't it? H'm, I know you had your head shaved
yesterday, so why do we need a dryer? My, what a lot of
questions we have this morning! The sponge – why is it wet?
Oh, to keep your scalp moist. As long as it's a snug fit,
don't you fret if it's a bit chilly – it'll soon warm up.

Well, that's it, we're almost done. Pardon, what's
that you say? You want to scratch – you've got an itch? Oh,
don't worry about it – it'll soon go away when I give the
signal to throw the switch.

Superman
(For 5 voices)

(All)   Zap! Pow! Biff! Bam!
           We think you're awesome, Superman!

(1)   Our comic-strip hero, heaven-sent,
           The mild, bespectacled, shy Clark Kent.
           Your true identity always concealed,
           The source of your power never revealed.
           You flatten gangsters with a punch
           And then take Lois out to lunch.

(All)   Zap! Pow! Biff! Bam!
           We think you're awesome, Superman!

(2)   Immune to bullet or blade of knife,
           You lead such a thrilling, adventurous life –
           A skyscraper blazing! People trapped inside!
           Screaming in panic! Nowhere to hide!
           You put out the flames with a blast of your breath,
           Saving thousands of lives from certain death.

(All)   Zap! Pow! Biff! Bam!
           We think you're awesome, Superman!

(3)   An asteroid of gigantic girth
           On collision-course with planet Earth!
           You fly up to meet and, with effortless grace,
           Send it spinning harmlessly into space.
           No-one need fear when help is at hand
           From the greatest protector in the land.

(All)   Zap! Pow! Biff! Bam!
We think you're awesome, Superman!

(4)   All the mobsters and molls had better beware
When you don your cape and take to the air.
By X-ray vision tracked to their den,
They cool their heels in the city pen.
Not even Lex Luthor would dare to fight –
A blow from your fist like dynamite.

(All)   Zap! Pow! Biff! Bam!
We think you're awesome, Superman!

(5)   *For the guardian of the universe,*
For the hero of the human race,
For the crusader fighting crime,
For the champion of truth and justice,
For the saviour of Metropolis,
Let's hear it one more time –

(All)   Zap! Pow! Biff! Bam!
We think you're awesome, Superman!

Boat

The oddest thing about a boat, I'd say,
    When one begins to row,
Is having to face the opposite way
    To where one wants to go.

But sitting thus would never do
When paddling past in one's canoe.

Journeys
(A whimsy)

Ask we might, if tipsy or contrary,
Why the longest mile is the last mile home,
If it's all that far to Tipperary,
And why every road leads onward to Rome,

Or what did Chesterton's old drunkard do
While boozily seeking his own abode,
But leglessly crash through a hedge or two
And make, when slewed, the rolling English road.

And despite any query we might have
About the sober line of Thomas Gray:
"The paths of glory lead but to the grave.",
Did his ploughman after a long, hard day,
Plod wearily homeward, as we would think,
Or trudge to the pub for a well-earned drink?

Earth

I am the haunt of badger, rabbit
And mole, centipede, beetle and worm,
The jay's acorn, skeletons of dead
Leaves, the ghost of mouse and vole.

My face turned-up by the plough,
Quarried and pocked in feature. Sunk
With oil-well, mine-shaft, a conduit
For water-main, gas-pipe and sewer.

I am cut, dug, gouged, bulldozed,
Graded and rolled, pile-driven,
Compacted, blown-up, extracted,
On commodity-markets bought and sold.

My skin with wheat and the land-mine
Is sown. I hide the arms-dump,
The mass-grave, the unknown
Soldier, the dog's bone.

I turn to loam hero and deserter, pope
And heretic, rich man and pauper.
The composition of your brain
And hand no more to me than clay or sand.

I am earth. I was here before you came.
I shall be here when you have gone.
Take care – you injure flesh when you sink
The spade. I bear the blueprint of blood
And bone. I am the soil of which you are made.

Air

I lift the bulk of the aeroplane,
The wing of the butterfly.
I am the oxygen in your blood.
Without me, you would die.

I form the gentle summer breeze,
The raging winter storm.
I bear the sound of the mother's pain,
The cry of the newly born.

I brought to Keats at twilight
The sweet song of the nightingale;
Carried the first gas at Ypres,
The scream of shells at Passchendaele.

I hold the scent of the rose,
The pheromone of the moth.
I am the first breath of birth,
The last of death.

I let fall the tear and the raindrop,
The warhead of the bomb;
Know neither good nor evil,
Right nor wrong.

I thin toward the edge of space.
I am heaven. I am sky.
I am argon, neon, krypton.
I am nitrogen and oxygen.
Without me, you would die.

Fire

I am fire - I can blaze;
I am fire - I can thrill;
I am fire - I can cleanse;
I am fire- I can kill.

I fled down the slopes of Mount Olympus
In the fearful grasp of Prometheus;
Burst through the cap of Krakatoa;
From Etna spilled in murdering magma.

I can singe – I can toast;
I can scorch – I can roast;
I can flash – I can flare;
I can gleam – I can glare.

I rained with smoking balls of brimstone
Upon Sodom and Gomorrah;
I burn incense on the altar,
The clothing of the leper.

I am fire – I can leap;
I am fire – I can run;
I am the white meat of the moon;
I am the red meat of the sun.

I withered the unworthy hand of Cranmer;
Melted granite at Hiroshima.
My fingers will run through paper and sticks
As quickly as the hair of heretics.

I am fire – I can spark;
I am fire – I can spit;
I know no self-control
When my passions have been lit.

I fired the boilers of the Flying Scotsman;
For three nights seared the <u>nights</u> of Dresden. *streets*
I am the ghost of a Jewish foot
On a flu in Auschwitz tacked in soot.

I am fire - I can blaze;
I am fire - I can thrill;
I am fire - I can cleanse;
I am fire- I can kill.

Water

I fell as rain on the first dinosaur.
I curled in Whitechapel mist round the blade
Of Jack the Ripper. Flushed down a sewer,
I carry a trace of menstrual blood.

Each day, unceasingly, my ripples lap
At the wall of the Hoover Dam.
I hang, a drop, on the mouth of a tap.
Freeze on the fleece of a stillborn lamb.

I sluiced gore from the block of Anne Boleyn.
I roll in the swell of the Atlantic.
Tinkle as ice in a glass of gin.
Shone with stars as I sank the Titanic.

In milk, I dribble down a baby's bib.
I am the raw tears of a sobbing child.
I leak onto a mortuary slab
From the drowned lungs of a suicide.

From stormblack skies in the Old Testament,
For forty days I beat upon the Ark.
And I splashed in naked excitement
As Archimedes leapt from the bath.

I squirmed under the microscope of Pasteur
In the slaver of a rabid dog.
Typhoid I may bear, and cholera,
Or lurk in a bank of Killer Fog.

I wetted with dew the grass of Eden.
Lay chilled in the egg of the dodo.
Turned white in the breath of Napoleon
On the long winter march from Moscow.

I am mist and cloud. I am frost and rain.
A crystal of ice in a freezer.
The sweat in your armpit. A scarlet stain
On the stabbed cloak of Caesar.

I rise in spray from a waterfall's roar.
I christen and bless on the Sabbath.
I am the raindrop that fell on the first dinosaur.
I am the snowflake that muffled the last mammoth.

The Lamp-post

Sometimes, beneath my light
In the cold of a winter night,
Lovers will stand and kiss;
And sometimes, caught in my glow
On the pavement below,
A stray dog bestow
Something less loving than this.

Strange Footprints

On the smooth,
flat stone of the
granary-floor, fluffed
and white with the dust of
wheat, lay the delicate prints
of a pigeon's feet. Slender, three-
toed and dark, each to the other
a mirror, they seemed with such
gentleness to have been
impressed that I thought
they were footprints
of angels.

Marijuana

Marijuana, hashish, or bhang,
Cannabis, ganja, or dope,
Are all made from hemp – a plant once used
To make the hangman's rope.

Steeplechaser

It broke a leg on jumping a fence,
Four furlongs from home in the race today.

To keep it alive didn't make much sense –
Considering, it seemed, the pounds and pence.

The vet was summoned without delay.
Shot in the head, it was hauled away.

Shap granite Boulder

I touch a rusted ring, an iron bolt
Sunk deep in a granite boulder,
And I see an old bull baited by dogs
On a hot market day in high summer,
Tossing its head in torment,
White eyes rolling in terror,
Crazed by the yap, snap
And snarl of cur and terrier –

But now, this afternoon of winter,
The bull and the dogs are gone
Like the baying crowd in its clamour,
And I stand alone in rain under grey
Sky and leaden cloud and finger
In silence the rusted ring, the iron
Bolt, dumb as the beast they chained
To the bonewhite granite boulder.

Horse-mart, Brecon

As dusk draws on day grows cold,
At the end of the auction, left unsold,
Old horses too long in the tooth to buy,
Hill ponies not smart enough to ride,
Appraised by the look in a knackerman's eye
For dogmeat, bonemeal, and hide.

Battery Hen

"Imprisoned in a metal cage,
　　Condemned to laying eggs,
My head stuck-out between the bars,
　　No room to stretch my legs.

"Stifled for life in a wire-cell
　　By artificial heat,
Never to feel the wind and sun
　　Or grass beneath my feet.

"But with ovulation failing
　　And egg-production low,
I must vacate the wire-crate
　　I held upon Death-row.

"Hung by the feet, electrically-stunned,
　　In the last blurred scene of my life,
I hasten by conveyor-belt
　　To an automatic knife.

"With head cut off, I quickly drop
　　Into a scalding vat,
To be boiled-down into pet-food
　　To feed some dog or cat.

"And that completes my sentence,"
　　Said a common battery-hen,
"My brief life spent producing eggs
　　Locked-up in a wire-pen."

Pig

Stunned. Stuck. Dewlap cut.
Slaughtered in its squeal.
Hot blood drained. Bowels drawn.
Hooked on a bar of steel.

Displayed in a butcher's window.
Neatly cleavered and sawn.
Reduced to joint and cold white lard.
Sausage, faggot, and brawn.

Animals

"Will no creature be left
In the world, one day?"
Sighed a thoughtful young girl
In a wistful way:

"No dog, no cat,
No mouse, no rat,
No fox, no hare,
No wolf, no bear:

Just people,
People,
Everywhere."

The Wishbone

My father would give – as a Christmas treat –
The wishbone of the turkey when he'd done
With carving into slices the white meat
Of the breast. My brother and I, in fun,
Would curl a little finger through the cruck
Of bone and tug until it snapped. (The one
With the longer splint of bone was in luck
And made a wish; the other's chance had gone.)
Whenever I won, I'd secretly pray
That my mother would never, ever die,
Nor that one night, distraught, would run away
Through quarrelling with my father, though why
I shall never know, because both have died
Long since; so that little forked wishbone lied.

If ladies . . .

If ladies at Christmas like poultry were dressed
    And cooked for a festive treat,
Their succulent thighs and tender breasts
    Browning nicely in the heat,
Would each feathered guest politely request
    When it comes to the table to eat,
Some cranberry sauce to sweeten the taste
    Of the delicate human meat?

Turkeys' Prayer

Protect us, Lord, on the turkey-farm
From all who mean to do us harm;
Guard us, we pray, from fox or stoat
And cut, instead, the farmer's throat.

Turkeys and the Magi

That three wise geezers had come from afar,
Led by the light of some 'eavenly star
(When none of them blokes never 'ad no car)
To us turkeys, like, seems a bit bizarre,
For they started Christmas an' all that blah,
With tinsel an' gifts an' such la-di-da.
P'rhaps, me an' my mates, we ought to say, "Ta" –
We don't think! – 'cos they made a right faux-pas!
To, "Merry Christmas!", we'd all gobble, "Bah!" –
The last thing we want is to shout, "Hurrah!"
(A word what's not found in our repertoire!).
When mid-winter's 'ere, we can say, "Ta-ra!",
For we ain't going to no Shangri-la
But just down the road to the abattoir.

Rhyme of the Christmas Turkey

Oh, it's lovely to be living here
   Upon the turkey-farm,
With such kind folk to care for us
   And keep us safe from harm.

But late last night, while sound asleep,
   We were startled by a scream –
One of the birds in pen Number Eight
   Had a most disturbing dream:

A nightmare so unnerving
   It made us catch our breath,
For we were seen as prisoners
   Being fattened-up for death.

She warned, "Beware of Christmas –
   It augurs naught but harm –
You are destined to be slaughtered
   Upon the turkey-farm.

"Prepare to be betrayed!" she cried,
   "By one you deem your friend.
At the time of the festive season,
   You will meet a brutal end."

As she spoke, we began to sense
   A feeling of alarm,
That perhaps our days were numbered
   Upon the turkey-farm.

But most of us dismissed the dream
   As really quite absurd –
What kind of fool would stoop to kill
   Such a fine and noble bird?

Oh, it's lovely to be living here
   Upon the turkey-farm,
With such kind folk to care for us
   And keep us safe from harm.

Without Me ...

Without me,
no bird would sing,
no tide be pulled,
no cow be milked
or dewdrop form.

No growth of marrow
in the bone,
no sun, no rain,
no passion wear the heart
or water smooth the stone.

No pebble break
a pool in rings,
no grief be eased,
no pain be dulled
or breath be drawn.

No autumn leaf
or petal fall,
no sound of laughter
or applause,
no last performance,
no bow, no curtain-call.

One hundred years ...

One hundred years this winter's night,
Should these brief lines again be read,
The stars will burn as clear and bright
As they do now, though I be dead.